ROCKY MOUNTAIN BIGHORNS

ROCKY MOUNTAIN BIGHORNS

Kay McDearmon

Illustrated with photographs
by DR. VALERIUS GEIST

DODD, MEAD & COMPANY
New York

To Dan and Chris

ACKNOWLEDGMENT

My special thanks to Dr. Valerius Geist, author of *Mountain Sheep: A Study in Behavior and Evolution,* for answering all my questions and supplying most of the photographs for this book.

PHOTOGRAPH CREDITS: Cincinnati Zoo, A Janet Ross Photograph, page 45; San Diego Zoo Photo, pages 31 and 37. All other photographs are courtesy of Dr. Valerius Geist, Environmental Design, University of Calgary, Calgary, Alberta, Canada.

1 2 3 4 5 6 7 8 9 10

Library of Congress Cataloging in Publication Data

McDearmon, Kay.
Rocky Mountain bighorns.

Includes index.
SUMMARY: An introduction to Rocky Mountain bighorn
sheep, discussing their physical characteristics,
agility, habitat, behavior, care and growth of the young,
natural enemies, and need for protection.
1. Bighorn sheep—Juvenile literature. [1. Bighorn
sheep] I. Geist, Valerius. II. Title.
QL737.U53M25   599'.7358   79-22902
ISBN 0-396-07791-9

FOREWORD

Long, long ago mountain sheep lived in most of the mountains of Europe, Asia, and North Africa. Later, wild sheep migrated over the land bridge then connecting Siberia to Alaska. They were the first wild sheep to appear in North America. That happened over ten thousand years ago.

Now mountain sheep are confined to the narrow arc of mountain ranges that stretch across southern Europe, Asia, and North America.

Experts currently recognize at least thirty-six varieties of wild mountain sheep. They range in size from a slight 80 pounds to a hefty 450 pounds, and they vary in color from snowy white to glossy black. The sheep also differ in the size and shape of their horns.

A Canadian Rocky Mountain bighorn in the snow.

In North America now there are two main kinds of wild mountain sheep—thinhorns and bighorns.

Thinhorn sheep are found mainly in the mountains of Alaska, British Columbia, and the Yukon.

Bighorn sheep have adapted to a wide range of conditions, from the frigid, blizzardy winters of the Canadian Rockies to the broiling heat of the deserts of the American Southwest and northern Mexico.

The Rocky Mountain variety is the largest and most abundant of the bighorn sheep.

A band of large rams on the range in springtime.

Early one spring morning a band of brown bighorn sheep was quietly feeding upon a grassy slope in the Rocky Mountains. Suddenly, an old female looked up. She saw a lean coyote moving out from behind a dwarfed fir tree. As the ewe stared, the coyote started streaking across the mountainside.

Almost instantly, all the sheep bounded off. The coyote, its bushy tail outstretched, raced after them. But before it could catch one of the lambs the sheep were scampering up a rocky cliff. The race was over, as the hungry coyote couldn't pursue them there.

Rocky Mountain bighorns can almost always escape from coyotes, cougars, grizzly bears, or wolves. The sure-

Coyote.

footed sheep can easily outrun these enemies when they can scramble up steep cliffs. And in the rugged areas the sheep favor, they are rarely far away from cliffs.

SKILL AS JUMPERS

On their hoofed and cushioned feet the sheep can zigzag across narrow ledges of cliffs. But they are best known for their remarkable skill in jumping.

Years ago American explorers started a legend that these slender-legged, muscular mountain sheep could jump off cliffs, land on their horns, and flip themselves over—all without injuring a muscle.

Bighorns cannot perform such miracles, but they are among the best and most graceful jumpers in the animal world. They regularly leap like acrobats from ledge to ledge. They seem to fly across chasms. And often they will jump off a cliff in their path.

John Muir, the famous American naturalist, tells of a band of bighorns that plunged off a 150-foot cliff, one after the other, and all landed perfectly.

Rams playing in early summer. One is jumping up; the far two are about to clash.

Size

One would expect such agile animals to be slender. Instead, the stocky bighorns that live in the Rocky Mountains of the United States and Canada (*Ovis canadensis canadensis*) are among the largest wild sheep in the world.

A full-grown male bighorn around eight years of age may reach 300 pounds; a few of the largest-horned males weigh more. Females are much smaller, but at their top weight of around 160 pounds, they still weigh twice as much as a European variety of wild mountain sheep.

Where Bighorns Are Found

Once, long ago, experts say that more than one million short-tailed bighorns lived in the mountains of North America. They were found from the Canadian Rockies to northern Mexico and east from the Cascades (in northern California, Oregon, and Washington) all the way to the Badlands of the Dakotas.

Early American explorers reported that bighorns were as plentiful in the mountains as buffaloes were on the plains.

12

A Rocky Mountain bighorn ram.

So it is not surprising that in Idaho a tribe of Indians known as "Sheep Eaters" lived on sheep.

Now bighorns no longer exist east of the Rockies, and only small pockets of these majestic sheep live in wilderness areas west of the mountains. Altogether, biologists estimate that less than fifteen thousand bighorns remain in the United States and Canada.

Horns

Pioneers, impressed by the massive horns of the Rocky Mountain male sheep, gave them their popular name of "bighorns." Unlike elk and moose that shed their antlers every winter and grow new ones in the spring, the sheep's hollow horns keep growing year after year.

The horns of an older male, or ram, can weigh thirty pounds and be fifty inches long. For over one hundred years white hunters (mostly men, but also a few women) have shot the larger-horned rams chiefly to display their heads as trophies in their homes.

As they grow, the rams' brown horns curl back and down close to their heads, and sometimes keep curling for

(Above) *Bighorn ram with broken horn tip.* (Below) *Female sheep.*

more than a complete circle. Female sheep also sprout horns atop their heads, but the ewes' horns are short and slender and simply curl back from their foreheads, so hunters don't compete for them.

No two sets of sheep's horns are identical. In fact, they are as individual as human fingerprints. Experts can learn much about a sheep's life merely by examining its horns. They can tell a ram's age by counting the age rings, but a similar count on a ewe's horns isn't as reliable.

The sheep's horns have an inner core of bone and an outer covering of a substance which is tough but not as hard as bone. Both rams and ewes seem to find their horns uncomfortable at times. To rub off the tips, they rotate them against shrubs and small trees.

Sometimes when a group of rams is resting one will stroll over to a stunted pine tree and rub his horns against it. This act alerts the other sheep, and in a few minutes all of them are on their feet rubbing their horns.

Even when two rams are fighting they sometimes pause to rub their horns against a shrub to try to remove irritating clumps of hair between their horns.

(Above) *Two rams. The one on right is nuzzling the horns of the other.* (Below) *Two rams. The one on the right is horning the face of the other.*

Two full-curl rams after fighting. The dark ram on left is the loser. His backing off is a sign that he is inferior to the larger ram.

FIGHTING

Bighorns fight all year round, using their horns as weapons. They fight to prove which one is superior. Ewes will butt another sheep with their spiked horns, but they rarely engage in long fights. Rams of about equal horn size often clash.

The smarter rams position themselves above their rival and attack going downhill, using gravity to increase the force of the charge. Now and then a sheep intent upon battling another will jump down upon him from a cliff.

Before they start hitting horns, the rams may shove and kick each other, growling as they lift their front legs. Then, as mountain sheep have always done, they follow a ritual or pattern.

Two rams fighting over the ewe in the photograph.

A clash between two rams.

The attacking ram rears upon his hind legs, inclines his head, and drops to all fours again. He rushes forward, and with all the force he can command, hits his rival a hard blow with the edge of one horn. Then he hits him with his other horn as well. The clashing of their horns can often be heard a mile away.

The fighting rams keep charging and smashing their heavy horns against each other until one of them gives up and walks away. This sometimes takes a long time. Once two rams fought—grunting and snorting at each other—

(Above) *An eight-year-old ram with broken horn tip.* (Below)
Bighorn ram on left in "low-stretch" to show he is superior.

for twenty-five hours. When they finally stopped they were exhausted, but neither of them had been badly injured.

Fighting sheep can escape serious injury because their horns act as shields, catching and softening the blows. The sheep's double-layered skull and thick facial hide also help to protect its head from damage. But many times horns break or splinter, and some sheep get broken noses.

A winner doesn't let a loser forget that it has lost, and may kick one that crosses its path. A loser shows it knows its rank by either turning away from a winner or even turning its snowy white rump patch toward it.

FEEDING

Sheep, of course, spend many of their waking hours feeding. They are herbivores, or plant-eating animals. They dine on grasses, herbs, sedges, and other low-growing plants and shrubs as the seasons and the terrain permit.

To help digest the dry, dusty plants it sometimes eats, a sheep has a stomach with four parts. From its mouth the chewed food drops into the rumen, the first cavity. There it is mashed into bits that the muscles push back into the mouth. After the sheep rechews the food, the other sections of the stomach finish digesting it.

In the Rockies winter snowstorms often prevent bighorns from getting the food they need. While seed heads and stalks remain above the ground the sheep bite them off. But when the snow covers everything the sheep have to paw beneath it to try to find food.

Sometimes they wander to the lower slopes in their search for food. There they may find little grass hidden under the snow, especially if cattle or domestic sheep have grazed in these areas earlier in the year.

Bighorn rams in December on a sparsely vegetated ridge 1½ miles high.

Sheep can paw through snow for food as long as the snow is soft, but in the late winter it often is icy and hard. Then the sheep favor the cliffs. There the stronger winds aid in clearing the snow, and the sheep can easily find any vegetation that is available.

Sheep digging in the snow for food.

Sheep on a 6,000-foot slope in May eating from a snowbank. Snow is the main source of water in cold climates.

Wherever the sheep are, roaring chinook winds that now and then race through the mountains help the sheep to survive the snowy season. These warm winds don't tarry long, but as they rush through they often clear vast areas of snow and expose the greenery.

PROTECTION AGAINST THE WEATHER

Bighorns are hardy animals. Those in the Canadian Rockies don't seek shelter in caves until the temperature reaches forty degrees below zero, and then mostly at night. Even on the open slopes the sheep's heavy coat protects it against the cold, blustery, wintry weather.

To keep warm the sheep has an outer layer of brown-tipped guard hairs and an inner layer of thick, gray, wool-like fleece.

Bighorns have heavy coats in winter.

One-year-old ram nuzzling horns of an older, superior ram. These sheep are also shedding.

As the sheep gradually sheds this double blanket in the spring, its dark brown fall coat may fade to a light yellow. And at times while the animal is molting, its hair hangs from its body in long strips.

To help loosen their hair, the sheep rub against rocks, trees, and small bushes. By midsummer they are bare-skinned. Meanwhile, mice have scooped up for their nests bits of the wool and guard hairs that have fallen onto the shrubbery. Over the next few months the sheep acquire another almost weatherproof coat.

LIVING AND TRAVELING TOGETHER

Bighorns live together in groups, or bands. A band may contain as few as five sheep, or as many as fifty-five. In the Canadian Rockies they select areas above timberline, and at times may share grassy slopes, cliffs, and canyons with whiskery white mountain goats. Everywhere the sheep seem to avoid forested areas, but they will take flight into the woods when cliffs are not close by.

Two large old rams in a friendly greeting.

Three rams trotting down a mountain slope.

Each band has at least a summer and a winter home range. The bighorns return to the same range in the same season year after year, but if hunters disturb them they will move elsewhere.

A band's home ranges may be close together, or they may be as much as twenty miles apart. In their summer travels—when the water isn't frozen or too cold—they swim across rivers or lakes in their path.

Whenever the wild sheep travel far they parade single file. Rams follow the one with the largest horns, while an old ewe usually leads the female groups. Leaders butt any sheep that tries to move ahead of them.

RESTING

Sometimes sheep rest on the grassy slope where they have been feeding; sometimes they climb to a rocky ledge overlooking the valleys and slopes below. All the band tend to rest together, but the sheep face away from each other. Like deer, they first drop down on their front legs, then on their rear legs. They tuck their front feet under their bodies.

The sheep settle down at times in hollow places that grizzly bears have already dug. More often they dig their own beds and paw the ground to remove the pebbles. Even

Sheep on a slope—mostly resting.

Cougar.

when they bed down among boulders the bighorns paw at the rocks before lying down.

VISION

Bighorns have remarkable daytime vision. With their large, amber eyes they can see a grizzly cub tobogganing down a foothill a mile away. Or they can sight a cougar coming silently up a far-off trail before it starts stalking a lamb that it might fancy for dinner.

31

When they see hunters some sheep will run up a rock slide or cliff and just stand there—safe from wolves and other animals, but a perfect target for the modern hunter with a rifle. But other sheep have learned to keep running, and sometimes they will plunge over a bluff to safety.

TAMING BIGHORNS

Scientists have only recently found that wild sheep—or at least those unaware of hunters—can be easily tamed. Only twenty years ago when Valerius Geist began studying sheep he donned white coveralls and wrapped a white towel around his head, pretending to be a mountain goat, so as not to frighten the sheep.

Later, when he was photographing bighorns at Banff National Park in the Canadian Rockies, he crept above the sheep so as not to alert them. But four sheep saw him, and they galloped up the slope and surrounded him. For a moment he looked up at them; they stared down at him. Then he lifted his hand, and to his surprise, a ram licked it.

Geist later learned that these sheep had been tamed by a park warden. The warden had offered them salt, which they

Dr. Geist's bighorn friends.

crave because their winter diet is lacking in minerals. Soon the bighorns were licking salt out of his hands.

The biologist used a similar approach to tame other sheep. At first he wandered close to them in the park every day for about two months. Then one day he offered the sheep some salt. At first they hesitated; then one strolled up to Geist and sampled the salt. Quickly, all the others did likewise.

In time the bighorns became remarkably friendly. One spring day as the scientist was looking through his field glasses, he saw one of his rams that had gone away during the winter. Geist waved to the far-off sheep, and he came racing across cliffs and gorges and halted in front of Geist to claim his treat.

When the scientist showed that he had no more salt, the ram made no move to leave. Together, the two climbed up a slope like the old friends they were. Finally, Geist left him with a group of resting rams.

Other bighorns at times reached into his pockets, followed him in the deep snow when he carved out a trail for them, and even lay down beside him for a nap. And the sheep didn't object if he removed ticks from their bodies.

MATING

In the Canadian Rockies the mating season begins in late November. Rams over two years old search for females that are ready to mate, and court them by showing off their horns. The rams also chase away smaller-horned males. This seems to please the ewes.

About six weeks later the males leave the females. Then before their lambs are born in late May the mothers-to-be go alone to separate sheltered areas near steep cliffs.

Large ram keeping other males away from ewe of his choice.

BIRTH

Ewes nearly always give birth to only a single lamb weighing about eight pounds. Almost immediately, the mother licks her woolly, mouse-colored lamb all over its entire body to dry it. Otherwise, her lamb could catch cold and perhaps even die.

Once the little lamb is dry, it struggles to its feet. As it stands on its still wobbly legs, it reaches for its mother's warm milk, and wiggles its bobbed tail as it nurses.

Afterward the lamb naps, cuddled up alongside its mother. Within a few hours the tiny lamb can play, and before the day's end it can run, though in rather clumsy

Bighorn lamb about six weeks old.

Golden eagle.

fashion. The next day it can follow its mother in short strolls around the rocks. And soon it can jump, without any coaxing from its mother.

In the rocky cliffs the lamb need fear only the golden eagle. The great bird circles the cliffs looking for a tasty meal to share with its hungry eaglets back in the nest. When it sights a lamb, it tucks in its broad wings and dives toward it.

If the ewe sees the eagle diving toward her tiny lamb, she tries to protect it. Sometimes she shoves it under her out of danger. Sometimes when the eagle is about to snatch her lamb she attacks the fierce bird with her horns, sending it soaring away.

Once in the Canadian Rockies a ewe was observed actually goring an eagle with her horns. The injured bird rolled all the way to the bottom of the mountain slope and never moved again.

MOTHERS AND LAMBS ON THE MOVE

Mothers remain alone with their newborn lambs for only about one week. Then they abandon their private hideaways and all the mothers and lambs settle together some distance away from the cliffs.

In July they move to their summer range. Here the lambs join the mothers' original band, perhaps in a mountain meadow bright with wild flowers. As the baby lambs approach, the females, yearlings, and slightly older rams in the band become excited and rush to meet them.

A ewe and two four-month-old lambs.

Lambs playing together around a fallen log.

PLAY

Soon the yearlings are playing with the little lambs. They gallop around boulders, slide down rocks, and leap from ledge to ledge. Sometimes they playfully kick and butt each other. Now and then a mother butts a yearling that plays too roughly with her lamb.

The lambs also play games. A few small ewes follow the leader up and around a dead tree trunk. Some lambs play "king of the mountain." One small ram climbs to the top of a boulder and tries to stay there while the others try to shove him off. When they do, another lamb takes his place and the game starts all over again.

Ground squirrel.

Mothers do not play often. While their lambs are frolicking, a few of the ewes may slip away and trot down the mountainside to a clay bank to lick salt. Sheep share such licks with elk, moose, mountain goats, and other animals in the area.

When a lamb goes exploring it may see squirrels scrambling up a tree or a marmot pop out of its den, whistle, and pop in again. But if the lamb wanders too far, it may not be able to find its way back. If it is lucky its mother will hear its frightened bleating and rescue it.

NURSING MOTHERS

A mother's concern is solely for her own lamb. She will not allow another hungry lamb to drink her milk. One time a little ram whose mother had injured her leg tried to coax her to stand so he could nurse. When she wouldn't, he tried to steal milk from another ewe. But each time the lamb came close, the ewe butted him severely.

Even when her own lamb is hungry, its mother isn't always willing to let it nurse. At such times the lamb swings in front of her and blocks her way with its body. Mothers always end their lamb's meal by pushing the little one away.

Mother lifting hind leg over lamb's neck to end nursing.

Gradually, lambs nurse less and nibble more grass and herbs. By late fall, like their mothers, the lambs dine entirely on vegetation. Thereafter, the mothers seems to lose all interest in their lambs. With food scarce in the winter a mother will sometimes butt her own six-month-old lamb away from her.

Some animals protect their young much longer than the sheep do. But the ewe has no effective weapon against larger animals or hunters with rifles. So both she and her lamb must rely on their speed and their ability to scuttle up rocky terrain to escape from danger.

GROWTH

The lambs grow fast. They start sprouting horns before they are three months old. On its first birthday, a female lamb that survives the often harsh winter weighs about sixty pounds; a male about seventy pounds. A year later the female's weight is likely to jump to about 110 pounds, while the male's soars to about 160.

Sometime after the rams reach their second birthday they leave their mothers' band and join a group of rams.

An adult ewe, a female and a male yearling.

Some female lambs also leave about this time and join another band led by ewes. Other females stay with their mothers' group all their lives, even though she tends to ignore them.

HAZARDS SHEEP FACE

Fighting isn't the only way bighorns can get hurt. Grizzlies digging for ground squirrels cause rocks to fall down the slopes. Big boulders break off from peaks in the spring, shattering into hundreds of pieces as they ramble downward. And huge snowslides at times cascade down the mountains, threatening to bury any sheep in their path.

The bighorns usually take these hazards in stride. When rocks start clattering down the slopes, or snow breaks loose from a ridge, the sheep look up, quickly move out of the way, and return to resting or feeding. A rock occasionally hits a ram's horn and breaks it, but the sheep seldom seem to get caught in snowslides.

All the sheep are pestered by lice, and at times tormented by blood-sucking ticks and mosquitoes. If the tick wounds become infected, the sheep may die.

Older bighorns have a special problem. As their front teeth gradually wear down, they have more and more trouble biting off grass. When their teeth finally drop out, the sheep can no longer eat and so they slowly starve.

Sheep, too, can starve when winters are severe or when livestock have eaten the grasses they need. Domestic sheep and cattle can be a hazard in another way. They can pass along fatal diseases to the bighorns. And the wild sheep also suffer from some of the diseases humans do, such as pneumonia.

When sheep leave the cliff areas, they are in some danger from other animals. Wolves, cougars, grizzlies, or coyotes rarely attack healthy mature sheep, but on occasion they do catch lambs and disabled or older sheep.

But by far the sheep's greatest enemy is man. Laws have ended uncontrolled hunting, but poachers—illegal hunters —still shoot many sheep. Livestock grazing is still allowed where some sheep feed. And roads and mines are invading the bighorn's habitat.

Grizzly bear.

LENGTH OF LIFE

With luck Rocky Mountain bighorns may live twenty
years. But few rams reach this age, partly because any over
seven can usually be shot during legal hunting seasons. And
many of the largest-horned rams that escape becoming a
hunter's prized trophy die much earlier than the females.
Perhaps this often happens because rams expend more
energy chasing females and fighting to remain leaders.

Bighorn rams in a huddle.

FUTURE

Much is currently being done by scientists and interested societies to improve the future of the Rocky Mountain bighorns. Scientists, for instance, have transplanted the wild sheep from problem areas to ones that better satisfy the sheep's needs.

But more could be done. Livestock grazing on the bighorns' ranges could be banned; further invasion of their ranges by man could be prevented. Laws could be improved and enforced. Then the survival of the magnificent Rocky Mountain bighorn can be assured.

INDEX